A Lift Of Wings

Kerry Darbishire

Kerry Darbishire.

Indigo Dreams Publishing

First Edition: A Lift Of Wings
First published in Great Britain in 2014, 2nd Printing 2016 by:
Indigo Dreams Publishing
24, Forest Houses
Cookworthy Moor
Halwill
Beaworthy
Devon
EX21 5UU
www.indigodreams.co.uk

ISBN 978-1-909357-59-4
British Library Cataloguing in Publication Data. A CIP record for this book can be obtained from the British Library.

Designed and typeset in Palatino Linotype by Indigo Dreams.
Cover image by Stephen J. Darbishire RBA.
Cover design by Ronnie Goodyer at Indigo Dreams.
Printed and bound in Great Britain by 4edge Ltd.
www.4edge.co.uk.

Papers used by Indigo Dreams are recyclable products made from wood grown in sustainable forests following the guidance of the Forest Stewardship Council.

For Steve, Rebecca and Naomi

"…the world offers itself to your imagination
calls to you like the wild geese, harsh and exciting –
over and over announcing your place
in the family of things."

From 'Wild Geese' by Mary Oliver

Acknowledgements

Poems have featured with Dawntreader IDP. Mslexia. Live from Worktown Anthology 2014. Ver Poets Anthology 2014. Here/There online magazine 2014. Poetic Republic 2014. The Interpreter's House. Forward Poetry 'A Way With Words'2014. Wasted – Runner-up Mslexia Competition. If I called them Words and Mungrisdale – Highly commended Mungrisdale Competition. The Hillside – Shortlisted The Charles Causley Competition. Rain – shortlisted Poetic Republic Competition 2014.

With thanks to Dawn and Ronnie at Indigo Dreams for Publishing my first collection. To Judy Brown for mentoring so brilliantly, her wisdom and having faith. To Andrew Forster and The Wordsworth Trust for their invaluable input and learning opportunities. To Dr Anne Mathieson – an angel. To Dr Geraldine Green for her true spirit, generosity and support. To Janni Howker and Ron Creer for their guidance and encouragement. To Steve for his love and patience.

A Lift Of Wings is Kerry Darbishire's first collection.

CONTENTS

A Lift Of Wings

Wasted

He'd signed in pencil on the inside sleeve
in a stained book I rescued from a damp box.
Origins of Some Naval Terms –
an account of ranks, uniforms,
    pay and punishment at sea.

I sunk my nose into pale amber pages
everything beginning with T,
tonnage, touch-and-go, to try
and he did but never quite managed
    to *heave to* in Mum's new world

after hauling in the drowned
off Crete night after greedy night.
Cast onto civvy street, he drifted –
scraped along on West End bit-parts
    and *snifters* in dreary afternoons.

I was Dad's favourite during his hopeful visits home.
Curled into his loose jumper
smelling of lanolin and Navy Cut,
I held his warm salt-cracked hands
    and ate his perfectly fried eggs.

One Saturday evening he took me for a treat;
happy with chips and Vimto on the bench
outside the Golden Rule, I waited and waited
until he emerged – pitched against the glass door skin-wrecked,
    strange hands on the wet street.

Rare Photos

I'm fifteen, looking back at the fells
their tops smeared by mist.
Dad is facing the lens, salient, reclaiming his prize.

I remember that day on the lake,
the pull and slip of oars in wide black water.
Our out-of-depth conversation

darted like pike in their dark homes
searching amongst embryonic layers
for each other. I can imagine how he felt

in those two hours of hire. I see it now – gold-framed,
his smile as uncertain as the void beneath our feet,
expectation grabbing the stained shore.

I'm wearing the silver leaf-brooch he gave me.
His paisley cravat is loosely tied inside a blue shirt –
the one he always wore for best.

First In

Every Easter we had a dare.
On the heel of winter's nip
  before trees budded
    and grass loosened,
we raced like hares.

Towels wrapped
our blancmange bodies, we shrieked
  and laughed bare-foot along the path
    knuckled with shale and willow roots
trying to slow us down.

River Brathay swirled white
from the valley top,
  pounded Skelwith Force,
    curled mossy rocks, glassy inlets
home to sticklebacks, then slowed

into a bowl – deep with eel and perch
slipped from herons' stab and baited pins,
  brimmed with woodland stir
    that caught and reeled us in
to Adam's Dub.

Hearts racing,
toes tingled the water-line,
  our hands locked in that moment
    knowing if one did
we both had to.

Sometimes we threw ourselves
sometimes we slithered in
  gulping air
    snatched from our lungs
like babies baptized.

In The Shadow of a May

She lay sheltered
from the Helm wind – stretched
like a pumping balloon,
hooves fidgeted air
    then still as a hearthrug.

Just like Ma Myers at Brow Farm
when I reached to spy through mullions
and saw her spined on milked-stone flags
flour-faced, hands cradling her swollen stomach.
    I fled into shadows of the byre.

This one dangles gluing her back-end,
eyes rolling white as clouds on Whinfell,
bleated me her secret. From a grinning mouth
under her tail – red oozed – dripped
    like poppies on the bedded turf.

I snapped a stick off the thorn in case, shouted
but no-one heard above the easterly
and George's mallet anchoring his boundary
with a cuckoo two fields away.
    I watched saliva spume her jaws

her stomach wrenched like a duffle bag –
gusts of tin and silo pinched my nose.
I dodged for sweeter air.
A burst of sun threw its blanket over her
    and with the slap of a boat in water,

the ewe slid the bag on the ground.
Gentle as her mother
she turned her head and with her tongue
untied the kicking bundle,
    let go a blood-wet lamb.

Mr Mounsey

Regular as our grandfather clock
his clogs flinted the road
keen as a horse to fodder – midday,
    everyday.

Trousers rat-proofed with twine,
pie-hat cupped to his heart,
salt-white head tilting the breath
    of quarries he'd worked,

tarns he swam,
miles he trekked to school
through snow drifting a valley
    he never left in eighty years.

Aye, we thort nowt on it in them days,

he told us as he sat on the ladder-back
at the edge of the sitting room harnessed to then,
his leather hands waxing the oak arms,
    his mind – sharp as slate.

On the Bridge

In our moment of promise,
lens open, finger poised
hinging past and future,
   we sit in warmth on the bridge wall.

Dressed in ideas and confidence,
we sing along to the river tune,
echoes of our callow vows
   wake bats in their swirling stone arches.

Boulder banks of fastened snowdrops
stormed from upland February gardens,
huddle like friends lost and found.
Our summers sleep in lanes and meadows,
   tree dens reach a slate sky

and we smile like cowgirls,
pop stars and mothers into the camera,
imagine the words to our dreams,
streaming threads of hope like north-bound geese
   leaving us woven into this place.

If I Called Them Words

Two rooms away I heard you, every night,
   songs of waking birds,
      rhymes of rivers in full storm,
         whispers in silvered trees.
That's how I felt when you played your piano.
   I held those warm sounds
wrapped them around me, fell asleep.
You didn't have the time to teach me
   so I watched your hands every day
      sure as nectared butterflies along the keys,
         so sure that I would find the notes to please you
if I sat up straight and smiled with my eyes closed
   and if I called them words, one day
I'd press them gently on the page.

The Night Dad took me to the Island House

named after beautiful Isabella,
we rowed across the lake
hunched against a January squall
slicing off the fells.
I imagined her boat

  silhouetted
on the moon-full water
easing off inky pebbles in the bay
where winter trees jigged
in the last lap of oars.

  Her cries soft as ribbons
slipped brocade coverlets,
in armoured bedrooms,
floors tapped like oysters
– iced

  and sash windows
higher than churches
fluttered like wings
amongst bony arms of red velvet
that banned light long ago –

  before naphthalene oozed
from the wardrobe –
bequeathed tweed suits stiffened,
before breath turned
the colour of a moth in winter.

The River Brathay

Runs like a flock of Herdwick
gathered from Langdale crags
   flows under pines, oak and hazel
shoulders bilberry banks
   swims Adam's Dub
carves through Skelwith
   nudges nose to tail round islands
rocks and boughed barricades
hoofing a steady rhythm under the bridge
   towards the pen of Windermere.

   I heave dams in damp-lunged air.
Wellies sluice, clothes suck
like plastic bags on bruised legs
   pooling deeper and deeper.
Dippers tap along margins of marigolds,
   Herons glide and tug away like kites,
trout weave green ribbons in gravel basins
against silver coins fizzing evening sun
until Langdale Pikes slowly steals them all.
Weak as twilight I'm hauled into bed –
   not even the Snow Goose keeps me awake.

   Morning pours warm over Loughrigg like syrup on sponge.
I count ten mud pies along the hen hut,
stack beech-leaf sandwiches at the water's edge,
a hungry traveller may buy them all
   the Queen may come to tea.
Saws whine across the bank.
Quarry men slice stone like ham
and water sludges a slow slate-grey
   as if the river has grown old in the night.

Bert rattles a bucket over his arm –
hands buried in mould-coloured overalls.
I watch him lurk by Blossom Field.
  His crow-shoulders hunch with each breath
and step towards his dust-dry shed with trays
of muck-fluffed eggs, some on their sides –
turned every day waiting for a broody;
  cornered barrels of seed, baler twine snaked
on rusty hooks, the stink of rats, dead grass
  and through broken glass, a cobwebbed view
of the Riley twins' bedroom window.
  His wife as blind as Brathay fog.

  September bursts balloons of milk
over Crinkle Crags. White ladies
  swell ghylls and swill the Force
into peat-brown soup from the pail of Elterwater.
Islands sink, oak masts reach
and rafts of trees, swollen sheep, garden chairs
  clutter towards Ambleside.
Gulls spike the sky, cry at the wind.
  Our blind dog hasn't come home for dinner.

  Evening softens in woodland mist.
Blackbirds chorus high in the pine cathedral.
Kingfishers dart like party streamers
  so tonight I make my bed under Dad's pine
where branches admire their reflection –
  balance a full moon on bowed arms,
whisper me into wolf sleep.
Beetles drip, spiders spin
and dawn shivers layers of damp through
  the prickly army blanket.

At first light Bob-the-fly
hobbles like a toad in cap and tweeds onto the bridge
   and opens his tin of fresh worms muttering about rain.
He hooks a wriggler
and with a hiss faster than a bike wheel –
   reels it into the current.
He waits, still as hunched rocks
flicks his rod like a dragon fly and hands it to me –
   breath held fast, I grip,
squeeze blood from my fingers
quick as a perch bite he cups for breasts
   I don't have.

And as the holidays slide behind
doors of unknown streets in towns,
I hear her notes – her slowing sound
   from bridge to dub, stone to stone –
Mum's hands stretch keys like wings of butterflies
caught in a breeze of Delius
   drifting evening water.

Paper lanterns burn orange and gold
up and down the river like a painting we've borrowed
until frost smudges earth pigments and snatches
   the landscape while our eyes are closed.
Lawns rust in leaves – like tramps with nowhere to go.
The lazy river glazes, waits for sleep and in the night
white blankets wrap round pines,
   fields and lanes drift in.
No cars pass by to see our snowmen.

Bertha is first to break the ice
to wash clothes with red-knuckled hands
she elbows in to buy from jumble sales.
   Jumpers, dresses, gabardine

she bags them all on handlebars
　　without a word, puffs up the hill.
No-one knows she mends –
thimbles hope into brown paper parcels
　　for those who live without.

　　A northerly slants smoke to south
from carriages of cottages,
lifts and drifts above the pines
　　and high amongst hard crags
wild geese arc a dawning sky.
February mist gathers the thaw
　　voice of a young year.

Across the River

Those summer evenings
  so easy and dusty.
We hung out on the village bridge
dangled our bruised legs over the drop
three – four solemn trout fidgeted
  amongst slimy rocks.

After a while when nothing happened
  we slinked over to Bob's bench
on the corner hoping for something
other than the smell of Edna's cooked vegetables.
We counted down the days for hours mouthing
  trailers for sale or rent

as one car purred by like a film star.
  We imagined Hollywood, silk blouses, love
and how that day would come.
Tarmac stayed warm and soft walking home,
sky slipped from the pines, smeared lipstick pink,
  a black bird sang across the river.

Finding Home

Her eyes were dim and skin drained the colour of rain
from gutter to hard ground offering nothing
and everything in a second. We stopped
under a jasmine-knotted porch
   nestled in cold stone.

The kitchen seeped long winters.
Flagged floors oozed lime and a tap
dripped away seconds that wanted to be held.
Tar-stained walls – old diaries whispered secrets
   through rooms we searched like candle-light

until we found a door into the back garden,
late sunshine snagged on currant bushes,
rhubarb spears pushed under the bones of a bench.
By a mossy wall
   we huddled in new warmth.

A Winter Gift

If the eggs didn't nudge each other
in the blood-warm bucket of water and they floated
to the top, we took them out. I watched twelve
out of fourteen fidget then sink like mint-white pebbles.

That first January

our present of two geese and a gander
from a farm on the coast, panicked over hedges –
flapped their new wings into Peter's field
as if migrating until we caught them
and they softened like air in our hands.

Amber beaks clattered, sapphire eyes pinned

the beginning of a story we hugged into a shed
of fresh straw. Henry, Gertie and Lucy discovered the river,
bagged the best lawns and on Valentine's day,
slipped moonshine eggs like secrets into caskets of down.

Henry became a queens' guard outside the sanctuary –

dressed in hissing armour, neck to the ground
patrolling inside to tuck in loose straw and roll back runaways
before they cooled. For twenty eight days they processed
to the river to drink, dampen breast feathers,

tend their caches while we prayed for no thunder to addle,

no drought and no hungry foxes. Come early May
our garden rolled in yellow like curls of butter over green plates.
Our years of scattering grain, opening and closing
their warm mornings and frosty nights slowed

until all they could do was trust and warn us of strangers.

Now in silence, grass grows undisturbed – even the river seems less useful and my cakes are pale.   On winter nights I reach into the cupboard inside a dark box soft with tissue and unwrap fabergé.

The Fell Wall
(2012/13)

Real as the westerly folded me
into the yellow scented fell side like a child
dreaming good dreams, I saw them –
    close enough to touch under a muscled sun
heaving scattered boulders side by side
farm lads – hefted pride coursing the winter line
from rise to set. Footings, throughs,
    cams like headstones to shelter ewes.

September sloped with tups raddled to their necks
in green, red and yellow, swaggering the flock,
proud as chieftains, worn as crooks against the wall, knackered
    as sunday morning waiting for the cart to take them home.
December held skeletal limbs in its spell,
set the New Year in wise words only to be broken.
March turned
    furious white – blinding the night.

Morning threw silence over lost land,
the fell wall was bound in waves of icy graves,
    sheep and lambs frozen to the ground.

Rainstorm

Sky blurs, lowers like a press.
Rain-drops group like lyrics
stamp the parched hillside,
turn sheep into boulders
  churn peat into becks
    dust to mud and soon in the yard

hens stoop to half their size
with feathers glued.
A gang of jackdaws swoop barn eaves
– cocky boys in shiny gear.
  Grass and buttercups sink in plaits across the field
    mice and leverets flush out

and won't stop at hedges scattered white –
blossom trashed like stirks have belted through.
Walnut buds jump to turf,
rafters leak, buckets fill
  gutters sing
    and ring like xylophones.

In walls of ivy, blackbirds
roof their hatchlings fat with worms,
lupins, monkshood, roses list like masts
in a herbaceous sea mist,
  afternoon
    is drenched in perfume.

Behind crinkled curtains of rain
we wait for slates to hammer out
a slower beat, for slugs and frogs
  to celebrate – dare to slip and dance
    like leaves along the path.

Wind

is the messenger who runs ahead of storms.
Wind is the rudder that steers cattle away
  from oaks he bends and shreds over rippling fields,

  stampedes gorse like horses,
hurls roofs and birds across the yard,
  devours fell gates and gaps the land.

  When he tires, he drifts about,
sucks heat from afternoons and breathes out scents
  he's found in bluebell woods.

  In July he's lazy, sleeps through the early morning haze
too hot and weary to carry valley hum from lip to ear
  and leaves the sun to dry our fields of hay.

  Wedged in deckchairs tilted to his circus in the sky,
we watch bears, whales and elephants parade a dome
  while sandwiches and hats are whipped away.

Portrait

The scratch of pencil dry
along my jaw
  curves
    rocks back and forth.

His sharp blue eyes dart
from me to board to me to board
  like a wren
    searching for a landing.

Books, frames and canvases
are stacked in years
  around this eaved room
    lit only by the north.

Turpentine – spilt, stained and layered
reassuringly deep. Still
  as a camera I must breathe
    like sleep.

Through the open window,
  I fly celandine meadows,
    jump crackles of becks cupped in moss,
lie in woods, wind flowers, bracken,
  soar through stained-glass blue mountains
    into endless sky

until sun, sun splits clouds,
props and shifts distance,
  hauls me back here
    to my leaden chair

aching arms and numbness.
Slowly I stand,
  move into his position
    and see myself.

Candle at a Window

(painting by Winifred Nicholson)

Why else on that night
was the candle placed
between you and the moon?
A signal to singing sands,
a message of love – prayer
or simply so inspired after supper
you had to paint the view?

A dish moon spills the bay
draws to the window only
to be halted by a flame that says
    stop   don't move!
With blues loaned from afternoon's sky,
reds stirred from evening's earth
you layer your canvas. The room

is unimportant except for the flicker
of a night-time companion –
egg yolk yellow – a reference
to the island? I am lost in this
and don't care,
all I want is to sit with you
in the tallow air.

At the Exhibition

The still life persuades me
along a balcony crammed with clay pots,
cerise geraniums bubbling into the yard below
where midday is fastened
    and cats curl.

My hands burn impatiently on an arched door
    to a stone-quiet room.

Sunlight cuts a table – peels lemons to such sharpness
they appear to float in the sea-blue charger.
Impasto napkins catch full sail in magenta bowls
and two glasses, naples yellow, wait like anchors
    grounded in an afternoon. Above

curious birds migrate walls the colour of the desert
    towards a kitchen door where someone

holds steaming moules marinière as if they are jewels –
a gift prized from salty rocks – glinting
like something I remember
that now unexpectedly
    lets in through my scarf – coat – skin

secretly bleeds my northern palette
    with a fragrant spectrum.

Behind me
snow sprinkles the marble-white street
where footprints deepen
and for a while a woman reflects
    with a hint of a smile.

Fallen Sycamore

A westerly sweeps through this place
but makes no sound except
a brush of memories
across the fell.
The giant who sheltered livestock
on a summer's day,
invited owls and thrush to nest
and children's play
lies gullying the ground
with useless limbs
and must of severed roots
carried on the wind.

The ship
that battled
storms and drought
has run aground –
lost the fight, is seeping
into sea. No more for her
to do – holding snow,
casting seeds or
catching light,
her bow is torn
and sinking
with the
night.

A Westerly sweeps through this place,
and makes no sound except
the sigh of passing life
in fleeting moonlight.

On Old Ground

Here, something like knees and elbows push up turf.
    Why should I notice? Perhaps because

I want to know about the woman
who lime-washed bulging walls,
swept flagged floors, drew thin floral curtains
on misty mornings, stirred oats on the stove
with tight-bellied courage in this wild spot.

I walk along their soft greening boundary –
an intruder catching drips of wild lilac
on my face – the promise of Spring.
I want to think of him snapping these branches,
a honey pot crammed with his hedgerow arrangement

offered to her dusted table.
I want to hear his bracken songs, feel warm
enamel bowls – the smell of yeast stealing out
into a baking yard.
I don't want to think about the frozen babies,

weeping of useless milk, hungry old winters,
perished hands like hawthorn roots cracked
by the beast wind, grazed overcoats lanolin-stiff,
snowed in week after week – year on rigid year
until there were no more children.

Here, the ghyll is peaceful, certain, until I stand still.

October Tapestry

More sky than sea is stretched
  from edge to edge
    with lawn threads.
      Grey slub dashes the horizon
        – a flotilla in running-stitch.
Gulls hitch and weave umber
  through white reels of silk
    rolling Dinas bay
      looping pebbles pale as mist
        trimmed with seaweed.

Bringing in the Shrimps

When the ground crunched like shells
and breath hung still as a frozen cloth
Les knew it was time. A man of land and sea
  – ate only what he could carry.

    Come on lad, he'd call

pulling my man from warmth into the November night
to drive along the bare coast road where people had done
with walking for the day, where trees curved
    like net-mender's hands.

Into the sift of salt-white pebbles they marched
abreast of the tide pressed dark far beyond shifting sands
and where the sea held its breath
    set their nets on the bar.

With half an hour to scrape shoaled gullies – timing the turn
just right then back with a catch of phosphorescence
  – a mass of heaven
    steering into the bite.

We laid white sheets in the moon-shine yard, set wide pans
of water on the stove. My children woke soft-eyed and
wrapped in blankets to watch the sacks of grey turn pink-gold
    in the boil – a spread of ancient tender swilled onto linen.

Mountain Fog

After I left you and drove back home along the rust-wet lane
my view across the valley was obscured.
A grey blind had saw-toothed
over gorse, bracken, becks and boulders.
I stopped the car, opened the window
to let thin cold wash through me.
I wanted to be swallowed into an embroidered valley,
lift your mother's blanket,
pull in minutes together I let slip.
I wanted to draw out the fear that stayed behind your eyes
day after day in my brother's empty room,
unwrap all the voices you kindled that winter.
I wanted to brush your old hair,
sun to comb the ground I knew.
I wanted to hear the sound like angels holding the earth
with outstretched wings
when you vanished
with outstretched wings
I wanted to hear the sound like angels holding the earth,
sun to comb the ground I knew.
I wanted to brush your old hair,
unwrap all the voices you kindled that winter
day after day in my brother's empty room.
I wanted to draw out the fear that stayed behind your eyes,
pull in minutes together I let slip,
lift your mother's blanket.
I wanted to be swallowed into an embroidered valley.
To let thin cold wash through me
I stopped the car, opened the window.
Over gorse, bracken, becks and boulders
a grey blind had saw-toothed
my view across the valley was obscured
after I left you and drove back home along the rust-wet lane.

Butterflies

The month she came to convalesce
slower, slight in her frock of embroidered linen
   draping crêpe skin,
rain drenched and cooled the August garden.

I helped her settle in and upstairs became a sanctuary
of lavender, sepia photos, vases of buddleia
   on the marble stand.
Each morning she woke with her entourage

driven inside to flutter dry air.
Fans of burnt-red – old gold – white tips –
   a trompe l'œil clustered the ochre walls
like brooches, fastened as her.

Between stretched hours of dusk and dawn,
they gathered to face the window
   feasting on warmth
waiting for winter.

The Spare Room – Dove Cottage

In the event of Coleridge coming to stay,

in order to hold back damp, Dorothy's solution

was to spread the walls with yesterday's

news. I see him, *this sweet primrose month*

wrapped in The Times, reading by candlelight

before flickering into Black Drop sleep

to dream of *dearest Sara* this night

when stars fell secretly too deep.

In the visitor hush of this upstairs room

I watch the window's backdrop of sorrel,

ferns unfurling, poppies in such gloom

craving sun beneath the thickest laurel

in her noon-long shadow – keeper of rain

this April day, his footsteps on the lane.

Christmas Blouse

After exchanging and opening our presents
we drank tea while Mum withdrew to her bedroom.
Half an hour later she emerged – a film star entrance
bejewelled in her Frank Usher blouse.

She wore it every Christmas Day as far as I remember.
Five large flowers – two at the neck three at the front hem
hand-sewn in silver and pink glass beads – frozen rivers
over fine black silk – a dark landscape

draping her moon-pale décolleté. Not my style
but how it cast her demeanour from a lonely tea by the fire
to dinner at the Ritz. We applauded, sighed with admiration
which she received like an Oscar before gliding

into the kitchen – sherry in hand – line-perfect
as she served roast potatoes and gracefully handed round
a jug of gravy over the glass swan filled with dates –
her mother's centrepiece.

The blouse now hangs – winterly
on the *just in case* side of my wardrobe,
waiting in the wings. I couldn't stuff it in a bin bag,
the warmth of her perfume, all of us together.

Mungrisdale

I follow the snake through the valley,

open my window for sweetness

and the lament of buzzards

   circling heather.

Flood boulders have tumbled

re-marking the hillside.

Sheep gait the beck

   like a silver cross.

Scots pines could be

old Spanish lace.

Darkness is stealing the skyline

   and November chases me.

My hands are iron

clamping the wheel,

it's much further than I remember.

For Sale – Pollenca

He opened the door into a lace-lit room,
photo-lined walls, a Madonna raising faith
above a left-over lunch table. We didn't intend
disturbing someone's afternoon on our last day.

The old man pointed this way and that, spluttered Catalan
in low revs, bent us over tracks of newspapers.
In a blue-washed bedroom ancient light fell
on an iron bed, one church suit

and two shirts hanging in the corner like brothers.
We failed to find a way behind his bull-dark eyes
and olive-crushed skin – how he could leave his burnt slope
of fruit trees, fenced clutter of hens, walls crumbling

under family voices haunting his defeat? Maybe his children
were city-slick now, cared little for life above the sea
and the last vine-wrapped figs he insisted on handing to me.
We felt our thanks and smiles not helping, his prayers

unanswered once more behind the planked door. Low sun
and the Angelus Bell walked us back over skin-smooth stone
like strangers, awkward amongst dignity, carrying his gift
wanting nothing more than to take it home

Post Card

You would love
   the looped road out of Esporles ribboning the hillside,
     torn pines laughing, gripped against dry-mouth drops
     and rocks all the way to the villa,

geraniums with open arms
   in terracotta by the bleached green door,
     bare feet smoothed clean under silver-fingered olive trees
     here, long before the stone terrace.

A cerulean pool where we eat, read, sleep, forget for nine days.
   Sometimes dogs barking their parched hours
     across the valley, cockerels who spur squares
     of hopeful dust, a cat like yours

curled in the shade of my heart
   and goat bells louder than children playing
     into a silence we were expecting.
     This shawled evening –

distant lights strung loosely along the bay of Palma
   four hours away, and here on the veranda stripped of words
     our glasses draining faster than the Spanish heat
     you would love, our first holiday you're not here to tell.

Her Room

Is a crow's shadow. Curtains hang
like broken wings. Carpet dank –
    a careless lipstick red rucked and stained.

I try to picture her on sunny afternoons,
doors open playing Schumann,
    making tea and scones for passers by.

Rose wall-paper peels like brandy snaps,
pink-budded stems – lost in winters
    of cobwebs and the paraffin stove.

Bin bags slip like snakes in my hand
along dust-ornamented shelves,
    bloomed photos of children,

stiff handbags –
Eau de Cologne – tissues sting.
    I want her forgiveness.

A car creeps by – a familiar voice
splits quills of light through the window,
    swirls around me – the room is alive.

Under a vast dome of stars, stuffed bags crust
with frost. Beyond the river, owls are calling
    along dark arms of fields and woods where she walks.

On Haystacks

After I'd read an extract
from *My Family and other Animals,*
I told her about our latest walk – the view
from Innominate Tarn, how mist crumbled
like biscuits in the wind as we sipped tea.
How Lucy dog leaned to sniff
the bite and Buttermere floated
like a white blanket in and out of the sun
towards the sea.
I doubt Wainwright noticed
how hard it was for young mothers
to push buggies over the rough path
around that lake.   A short walk for some,
for us, the trek of shedding
four brittle years in one day –
as if we could.
       We tried
to convince the nurses
that at home was best, safe,
familiar after fifty four years.
We nailed down rugs, moved chairs,
taped lino from sitting room to bathroom
an easy route – short – no steps involved.
But they failed to believe
that she could manage blind.
       Just before she slept,
she squeezed my hand like summer
navigating every gully, stream,
ferned rock up there and whispered,
   one day a snow goose reeled through low clouds
as near as I am to you.

On that Starry Night

You lay in feathered paleness –
elegant as a swan on the river – gliding
towards the edge of a waterfall.
I waited by your window
   in silenced prayer.

   Across the valley gold sliced warm curtains,
spilled out conversations – once ours.
I wanted to show you sheep
bedded like boulders in wet grass,
   ebony tracks of startled deer

   and tell you how an owl shadowed pines,
snatched sharp air like food
in the snare of winter
when a lift of wings
   changed everything.

Snow

No stars, no shadows cast,
no breath
to blow out the porch candle.
We close the curtains on a range-black sky
and lie deep in feathers.
Snow falls like down in our sleep
packs the slates,
    wraps blankets around the house walls

with the silence of a sorcerer.
In the morning, apricot gloves slip
warm on the ghyll trees
as we push up Calf Fell.
Scarf breath tightens,
our hearts thud and wellies cake white
with each sinking tread.
    We watch jackdaws gang

and dart the distance,
a cockerel quivers the valley
firing his importance and dazzle.
Rowans drip diamonds borrowed for the night,
gorse statues spring to life, greet us –
their hats tip and fall.
Spoor lingers on a mat of tangled stubble,
    deer have moved on.

Rain

The sun might catch me early
  digging the fell side iced
    sliding like glass amongst gorse rags
the tang of lanolin
  dripping and tipping winter-blonde grass.
I will strip the heat of yesterday
      like darkness
        then lean and fall
      into the beck
    make music
 swirl
my soggy skirt through night-tangled roots and rocks
re-tread the musk of dead leaves and bird skulls
remember how last year we danced breathless
    I'll flinch chaffinch nests
      in the pine
        fox-blaze
    scraps of mist whisk them
out of reach
      drag
the winter hat off Coniston Old Man
drench Eileen's milky sheets
  nudge snowdrops
    'till honey spills
spread February-dead intakes with pins
  sparkle fleece-threaded wire
glean charcoal shadows
  clean to midday
and just before evening falls
 I will stand
with rainbow hands.

Picture the Leanest Time

Whinfell valley stretched

under February sheets sleeping off the crops.
Thin blankets of silage track fields into folds
of sycamore, ash and oak
where startles of Fieldfare search
in hope of breakfast.

Flakes begin to fall.

Silence is stolen by dogs barking across intakes.
The old man cough of sheep with gunged lungs
starving and scratting their way through gorse.
The early Edinburgh to London
slicing the valley in two.

See how arms of smoke

signal waking farms, yesterday's open-mouthed walls,
lambs unborn so far this year, hefted lads
wielding billhook and stakes,
laying straight tomorrow's margins
along and along ahead of sap and stir.

Leaving

I walked the lane into a different day.

November was letting go in silence,

air tightening an eerie sharp edge.

  I heard a final conversation –

crackling like a fire in the oak.

Burnt leaves curled stiff as ancient skin,

split from sap and bones into the earth

  sinking another season.

In the shredding rafters,

the lament of a robin

slipped like flecks of ash,

  followed me to my door.

I was ironing shirts when I got the phone call

I found him in the next town – north
   along corridors of paced vinyl
behind curtains so dim
they reminded me of boarding houses
   I stayed in as a child.

Morphine-pale he lay
   like an unwanted doll – legs twisted,
hands plastic in mine.
I stumbled in borrowed conversation,
   hung in laboured hours

waiting for his survival.
   And in a swollen river of thoughts
I clung to our easiness of yesterday
not thinking I would dream the summer back
   or wonder why.

I didn't cry,
   out in the wet Carlisle dawn
along grey strap-streets tightened by the eastern sky,
driving our abandoned car like a thief
through the M6 spray, into our lane – silence,
   ice-smooth sheets.

Her Winter Curtains

I mend the frayed hems and think of her

drawing back these velvet curtains on a crisp
February morning, inviting the palest sun to search
amongst chairs, tables, lamps and last night's ashtrays.

It's Friday, she will choose plaice
from the back of a van, from ice – melting
into wooden trays splayed with yesterday's catch.

I've almost matched the green thread needed
for the curtains – fern-dark, soft as a mole in my hands
– pink – deft as hers clinching the Times crossword.

Cigarette smoke curls polished air, a clock
drips out the afternoon, earl grey tea rests
in best china as she funnels letters into neat rows.

She taught me how to sow seeds,
prick out, harden off, pot on bold plants,
arrange flowers on the window sill

overlooking her garden jewelled with lilies
and roses sometimes the colour of the moon.

When I was a Bird

Once I was a bird   like a leaf   drifting

above everything that wasn't important

I couldn't feel flesh   except yours.

Star-sequinned nights   melted

into pink veins   stretched   further

because you gave them to me

and tasted   pure as a spring

surprising   somewhere   wild.

Junipers   crossed   horizons

and danced   on a limestone scar

with wild geese   woodcuts

you promised to complete   pinned

above my head

before you left.

I flex my feathers   wait

for your breath.

A Full Moon

Remembers and mourns her precious silver,
swell of angry tides, the shining price that weighs
so heavily inside her round door.

Tonight she moves slowly, slips space
across my lawn like a fox, paces a birch coppice
where boulders stubborn as memory trench a river.

There she stops, watches her reflection yaw
and shatter in the lash of November. Ripped limbs,
blooded leaves fall like lambs in the shadows of gardens,

children sleep in blitzed bedrooms;
above silent tables, the gutted stench
of a night that neither she nor rain can drench.

Escape
(On Reading the Mind Reader by Richard Wilbur)

Sun strikes lime through layered walnut leaves
their perfume dismissed by the breeze.
I lie in my hammock on a July afternoon
cocooned between his words
and an empty glass;
    some things are truly lost.

Gradual warmth flutters the pages I turn and turn
settling in like this glorious summer.
Someone has marked
A Black Birch in Winter (I like that)
underlined *the rifts, roughened surface*
   and *finished wisdom in a shrivelled skin*

as if I wouldn't notice
old trees are doomed to annual rebirth.
Observe the sap-glint, bud-swell,
how sparrows glide without fail
from branch to branch,
    hold their flute song

long after unscored notes have faded.
Disregard the withered bark, escape
with me into his last line,
Ah, you have read my mind.
One more perhaps...
    while shadows scatter.

The Thrush, The Wren and the Shrew

We float in formalin
in old coffee jars – lined
  along the shippon window ledge,
    our eyes pinned to a dull cobwebbed wall.

Occasionally she comes to look,
swirls us around to a fresh view
  – the slow line of hills
    where we sang away the summer

but now our feathers, fur and voice are numb,
December closes like cattle in the barn,
  thumbed blankets of mist
    press a whole apple orchard dreaming of blossom

and lambs, no bigger than us
slowly turn to face the same slate sky
  so still
    turbines are barely alive.

In These Walls

Tonight two owls call the dark, take turns.
I listen to their young cries and my heart leaps to a summer

where love lay secretly wrapped in new warmth
at the far end of the damson-dark orchard.

We abandoned our clothes on the stone table
and as morning sneaked through ripening fruit I dreamed

of the day you first walked along the lane to this house
to paste horse hair and lime onto oak laths.

You spoke in silence, waistcoat rough as heather
brushing my skin. I watched your earth-worn face

mortar-burnt hands pause in this place, the way
you looked at me – soft as evening light

a light that falls into notches in beams and walls,
seeks out chiselled hieroglyphs, restores something lost.

My fingers blindly skim the layered surface and stop
in the imprint of a hand, a key in a lock.

The Valley of Lost Farms
(Mardale)

Seventy five locals filled the church that last day.
Hymns and prayers spilled into August sunshine
and beyond six gnarled yews, crowds stood like haystooks
    in the meadow to say goodbye.

Heads bent to their soil – dry-walled plots
where hefted flocks had grazed
from Goosemire to Chapel Bridge to Riggindale
    summer, winter, seed and crops.

They spoke of gatherings at the Dun Bull Inn
– *for t' crack and ale* after shepherds' meet, the spinning
and knitting by firesides, the barking dogs that rounded
    stock to lambing to shearing – chivvied into yards,

honey-perfumed lanes, a first kiss,
the cuckoo, the wedding bell ringing thickets,
mayflowers and the cry
    from a first born in the bedroom facing east.

Up High Whelter the schoolyard rang with playtime –
clogs ran like bullocks, wild raspberries stooped
to the wind and snares lay slipped by the beck.
    Before the drowning

I heard exhumed coffins were strapped
and carted all to Shap – the pulpit
the weather vane and Mardale bell
    cast from Carlisle, to Rosthwaite.

Two standing stones on Bampton Common
now lean in turf like old-timers jawing
over a bowl of moon-limed farms
    brimmed with sky.

Songwriter

I'm in love with this place
    its snow, storms, those promising stars
and the way after last night's frosty grip
    the stream cuts like steel
between the fell wall and the ash tree.

The scent of moss drips notes so sharp
    and clear I want to drink. And here
the smooth pentatonic hum of a bee
    loops and keys into celandines –
rises and falls across the silk blue-violet valley

where one summer years ago I stood
    with my arm around you in belief – swayed green
on singing ground. But how the ash leans now,
    girth-wide – gravel skin – slow to let go
this season's prose from ink-stained finger nails.

Reflection

On the slant of a hillside heeled
with birch,
  pine
    and oak,
      umber bones link
      lean cautiously
      balance chandeliers
  like acrobats rehearsing
in the early morning glint.

A magpie cackles
reverbs the hollow
  battles territory
    rattles crystals
      to the ground.
      A heron rips air above my head
    wraps me in scent of moss and grass
  oozing last night's rain
enough to start a song in the wood.

Old wall cams hunch like toads
set to slide leaf-mould and fern-tangle
  to breeding waters where
    a bass chord of traffic rumbles
      alongside the hungry jaws of Grasmere lake
      eating trees
    cottages
  and the whole of Silver Howe
in one calm bite.

Winter Tracks   (Haiku)

Days grow weak as boughs
dip heavier with apples
   sweetly scented air

                Above faded land
                the wild geese fly south again
                   wood-smoke barely moves

December returns
stirring storms on mountain tops
   footprints in the snow

                Full moon on mountain
                Singing in a winter sky
                   falling stars on tarns

Landale's slate-sharp nights
soften over Skelwith Force
   waking heavy pines

                Woods shadow the land
                still as tribes biding their time
                   I am not alone

Sunlight seeks out tracks
of moonlit hare, deer and stoat
   running clear away

The Hillside

A bone-dry devil-of-an-easterly whistles
off the Howgills, sneaks under planked doors
leaches every blade and muscle
bending into rows of winter fodder.
    They call it the Helm wind.

It made for thin shelter on this slope
when the last son and his wife worked the farm.
Less snigging to be done – to carry into their oil-lit room
fumed with fresh hawthorn and steaming oats
    stirred on the iron range

that never went out to let bad luck in.
When she heard his distant hollering
and bracken whisper as the dog circled high intakes,
she knew he was watching sun spread the bay
    with a silver cloth and set her table

and waited for the pounding grey line
of ewes to stream by the pantry window to lower ground,
boot-scrape on stone flags,
his warmth on her neck, before the wind stole it,
    before limed walls sunk to moss and mist moved in.

Last Night

I walked the same tracks made in younger winters
and felt much as I did that first time.

Alongside the frosted garden wall, my collie ran ahead
into the field swept grey and tasteless.

Pearl light was slipping, air sweet as a forest
and the west burned red seeping to a southern magenta.

A few birds chattered themselves into a sleeping ghyll,
into moments of silence – beyond my life.

Foxes set up, marking the night, dog crouched close.
I followed their cries like the second hand of a clock

along the curved northern sky-line
over the Eden edge, imagining their hungry silhouettes.

A breeze nudged me,
a message I could so easily have missed.

Treasure

A treecreeper inches up the weather side of a sycamore,
taps mapped moss with the precision of an archaeologist.
Sunlight flicks wet branches switches lead grey and brown
to lime and orange like impressionist paintings that spring day

  at the Guggenheim.
     We lingered in the dawn – midday and dusk
       of Monet's haystacks – in each other, talked all along

  6th Avenue to Macey's.
     I didn't tell you I got vertigo
      on the glass escalator in the Trump Tower

but my
     how the bird's-eye view seemed as if the rest of the world
      would always be stretched in graphite.

Hydra was a meditation.
    We flip-flopped through oven-hot streets.
      You held my waist like flowers, my heart raced and later

we watched the western sky catch fire and smiled
    to think that swallows darting through medieval arches
      might have summered in our barn.

Do you remember driving from Malaga
  into the hills of Iznájar? We left the ocean smooth
    as a sheet pulled up sharp to the rocky coast,

through vineyards – villagers' main arteries drilled deep
  in sweeping arms burnt and bent against the wind.
    Olive trees like fathers, leaned into houses
      and plump fruit – children ready to take off

Now, in between late bursts of sun,
sleet wakes the hard earth – digs in.
I close my eyes, sleeping with the past,
the details buried in warmth.

Indigo Dreams Publishing Ltd
24, Forest Houses
Cookworthy Moor
Halwill
Beaworthy
Devon
EX21 5UU
www.indigodreams.co.uk